Ginger

Activity Book 3

Allgemeine Ausgabe – Neubearbeitung
Lehrwerk für Englisch ab Klasse 3

Erarbeitet von
Kerstin Caspari-Grote
Ina Grandt
Birgit Hollbrügge
Ulrike Kraaz
Claudia Neuber
Christel Simon
Ines Völtz

Cornelsen

Contents

Symbols

read	listen (CD 1.24)	act out
talk	draw	tick
write	cut	123 number

◊ In der Verkaufsauflage ab Frühsommer 2013 finden Sie hier Seitenverweise auf die Lehrerhandreichung.

What's your name?

1 Read.

2 Write.

3 Draw.

Good morning, Ginger.

My name is ______________________

Our ship

1 Talk. Read.

2 Colour. Write.

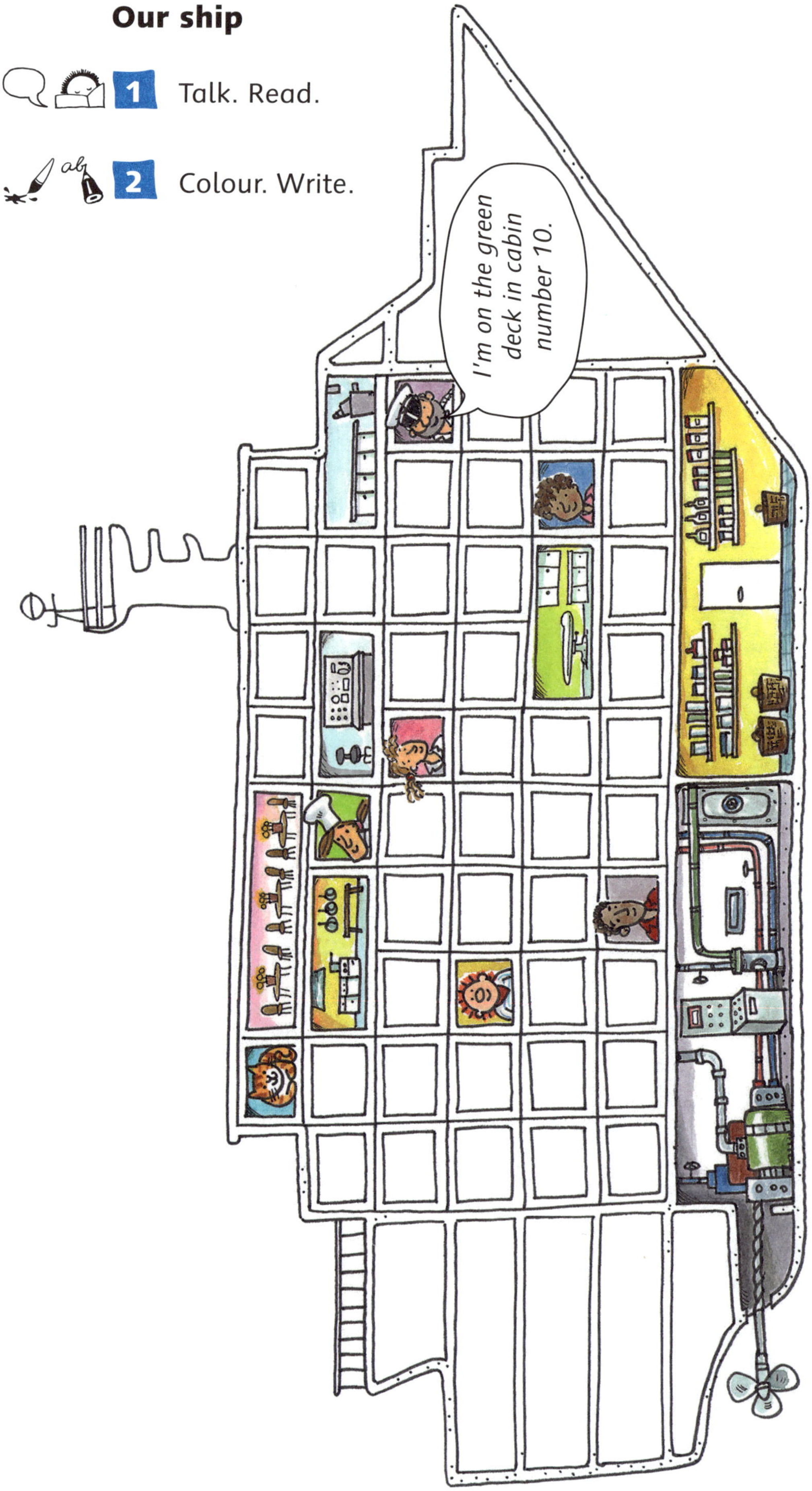

Ginger is on the orange deck. Captain Storm is on the green deck. Ginger's cat is on the blue deck.

Colin Baker is on the yellow deck. Debbie Jones is on the green deck. Dr Heal is on the red deck.

Ravi Metha is on the brown deck.

And you? I'm ______________________

Portfolio: My family photo

1 Draw. **2** Write.

my mother
my father
my sister
my brother
my grandfather
my grandmother

______
______
______

Portfolio: My packing list

1 Draw. **2** Write.

My packing list

______
______
______
______
______
______
______
______
______

Portfolio: My cabin

1 Draw.

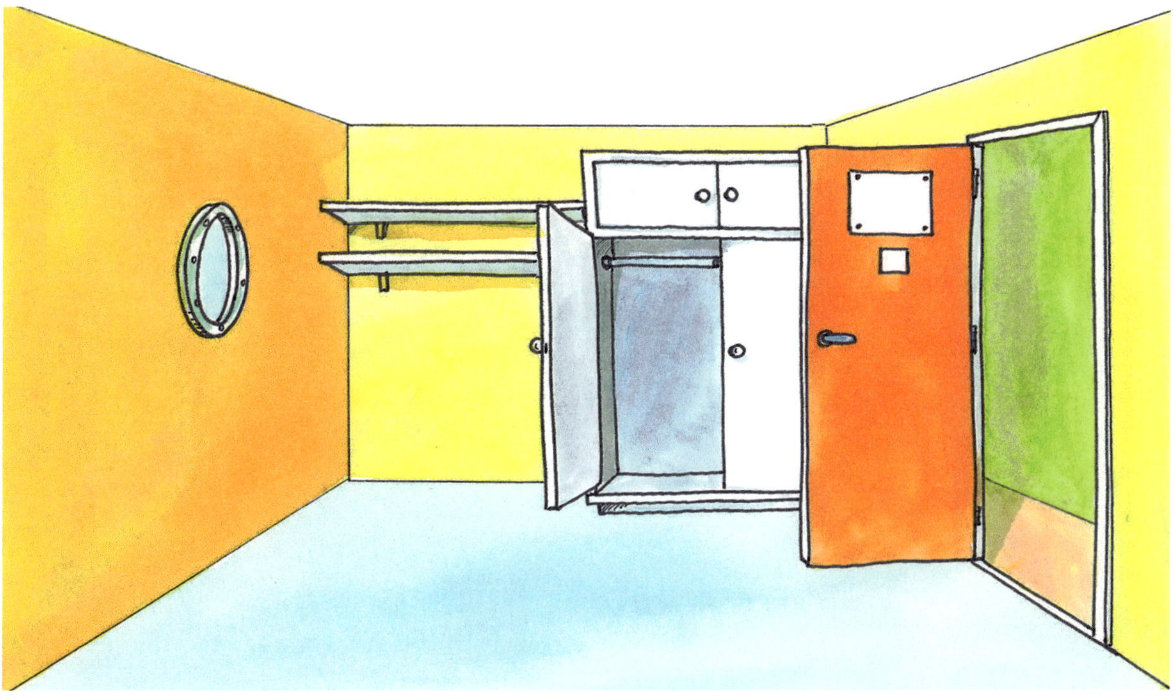

Portfolio: My boarding card

Name

From

Hair

Eyes

Deck

Cabin

Seine Kabine einrichten und sagen, wo sich verschiedene Gegenstände in der Kabine befinden; eine Bordkarte lesen und ausfüllen (◊)

Portfolio: My cabin

1 Read. Colour.

green	yellow
brown	orange
blue	red

2 Write.

My cabin

____

____

____

____

____

I like my cabin.

hammock

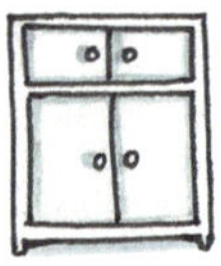

wardrobe

shelf

bed

chair

table

book

window

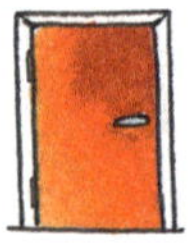

door

Portfolio: My boarding card

Boarding card

Ginger's action rhyme

1 Read. Write. **2** Act out.

my big tummy
my long T-shirt
my nose
my red hair
my round face

Ginger's action rhyme

I've got a round, round face,
and red and spiky hair,
freckles on my nose,
and I often stand and stare.

My shirt's too long,
my tummy's big and round.
When someone tickles me,
I jump right off the ground.

Breakfast tables

1 Talk.

2 What's missing? Write or draw.

cornflakes • bread
egg • honey • milk
orange juice

In the storeroom

CD 1.26

1 Listen.

2 Write.

3 What else? Draw or write.

Fruit

123 **1** Read and number.

apple • banana
grapefruit • lemon
orange • strawberry

2 Write.

Can I have some

____________ ____________ and some

____________ ____________, please?

____

____

____

____

Saftgläser nummerieren, Fragen vervollständigen (◊)

Favourite ice cream

1 What's your favourite ice cream?

Name								

__________ is the favourite ice cream in class __________

Colin's fun food

1 What's your favourite fun food?

2 Circle the words.

power flower

bread jam milk cornflakes egg chocolate orange

orange juice banana apple lemon grapefruit ham

strawberry cheese cucumber lettuce tuna tomato

cucu-boat

grapefruit monster

Portfolio: My fun food

1 Draw your fun food. Write a shopping list.

cucumber

lettuce

bread
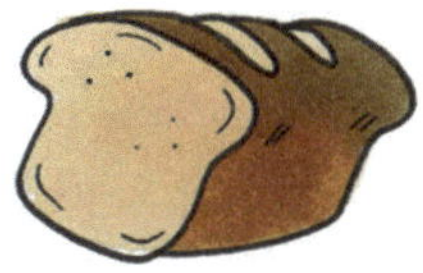

strawberry

banana

lemon
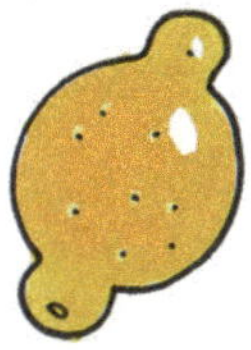

____

(name of my fun food)

ice cream

apple

tomato

orange juice

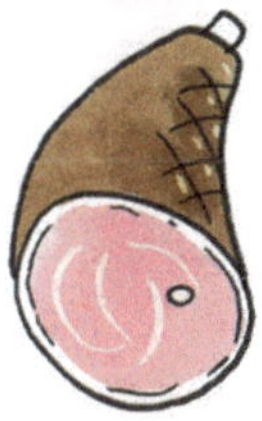
ham

tuna

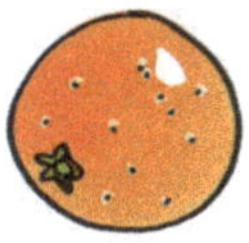
orange

cornflakes

milk

____

____

____

____

____

egg

jam

grapefruit
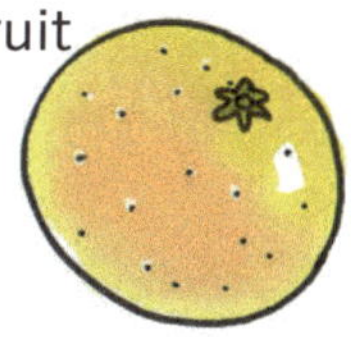

chocolate

vanilla

sandwich

cheese

Ein eigenes Gericht zeichnen und die verwendeten Zutaten aufschreiben (◊)

Orange Island

Was ich dazugelernt habe

Datum: ____________

Zeige jetzt noch einmal, was du kannst.
Ich fand die Aufgabe: ☺ leicht 😐 mittel ☹ schwer

◯ **1** Ich habe (Name) ____________ den Chant „On Monday no cornflakes" aufgesagt. ☐

MONDAY
TUESDAY
WEDNESDAY

THURSDAY
FRIDAY

◯ **2** Ich habe (Name) ____________ nach der Lieblingseissorte befragt. ☐

(Name) ____________ Lieblingssorte: ____________ .

◯ **3** Ich habe (Name) ____________ mein „Fun food" präsentiert. ☐

◯ **4** Ich habe (Name) ____________ die englischen Wörter für diese Früchte genannt:

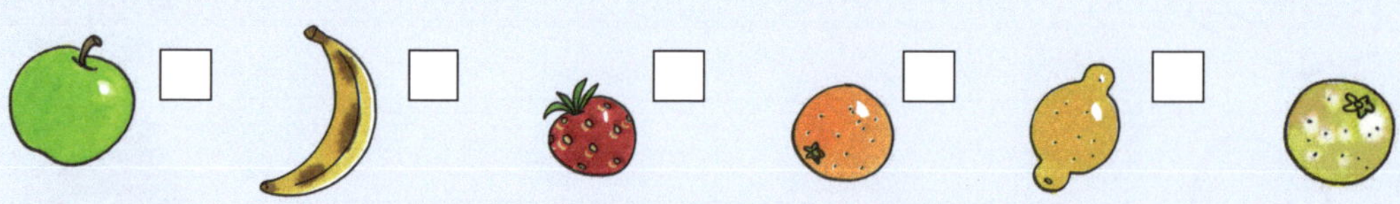

☐ ☐ ☐ ☐ ☐ ☐

◯ **5** Ich habe (Name) ____________ befragt, was er/sie auf einem Sandwich mag:

☐ ☐ ☐ ☐ ☐ ☐

My favourite breakfast

1 Draw.

Mr Ringley's circus: the pictures

1 Talk. Cut out.

Mr Ringley's circus: the story

1 Read. Glue the pictures.

Mr Ringley was happy in his circus.

The clown said, 'Bye-bye, Mr Ringley.'

The elephant said, 'Bye-bye, Mr Ringley.'

The juggler said, 'Bye-bye, Mr Ringley.'

The horse said, 'Bye-bye, Mr Ringley.'

Mr Ringley put the message in a bottle.

Sätze lesen, Bilder in der richtigen Reihenfolge einkleben (◊)

Animals

1 Write.

2 Draw.

bear
elephant
horse
lion
monkey
parrot

My favourite animal

bears
elephants
horses
lions
parrots

1 Write.

2 Talk. **3** Tick.

What animals do you like?

I like …

Name						

Funny clowns

1 Talk.

2 Draw.

3 Write.

1

The clown's ____________ is green.

2

The clown's ____________ is red.

3

The clown has got his __________ in his ____________.

4

The clown has got his __________ on his ____________.

nose • mouth • leg • toes • hair • ear • finger • nose • feet

Ein Partnerdiktat durchführen; Sätze vervollständigen (◊)

Portfolio: My circus act

1 Write and draw.

(name)

(act)

Was ich dazugelernt habe

Datum: ____________________

Zeige jetzt noch einmal, was du kannst.
Ich fand die Aufgabe: ☺ leicht 😐 mittel ☹ schwer

◯ **1** Ich habe (Name) ____________________ den Chant „Five in the circus" aufgesagt. ☐

◯ **2** Ich habe (Name) ____________________ nach dem Lieblingstier befragt: ☐

(Name) ____________________ Lieblingstier ist:

◯ **3** Ich kann diese Wörter für Tiere im Zirkus auch aufschreiben:

____.

◯ **4** Ich habe (Name) ____________________ mein Portfolio „My circus act" präsentiert. ☐

◯ **5** Ich habe (Name) ____________________ die englischen Wörter für diese Körperteile genannt:

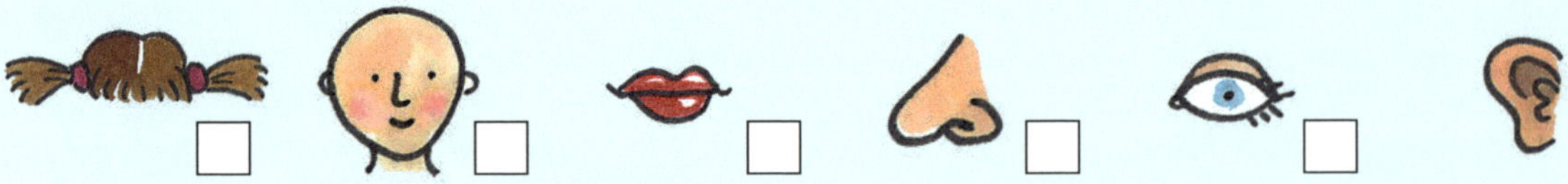

Ich kann einige davon auch aufschreiben:

____.

◯ **6** (Name) ____________________ und ich haben uns gegenseitig mit den Minibildkarten *Actions* fünf verschiedene Anweisungen gegeben und diese auch durchgeführt. ☐

Captain Storm's weather chart

1 Talk.

cloudy • cold • foggy • rainy • snowy • sunny • warm • windy

2 Write.

Monday cloudy, windy, cold

Tuesday ______________________

Wednesday ______________________

Thursday ______________________

Friday ______________________

Saturday ______________________

Sunday ______________________

A walk around the island

1 Read. Write. **2** Number. Talk.

☐

a mountain
a picnic
grass
a river
mud

☐

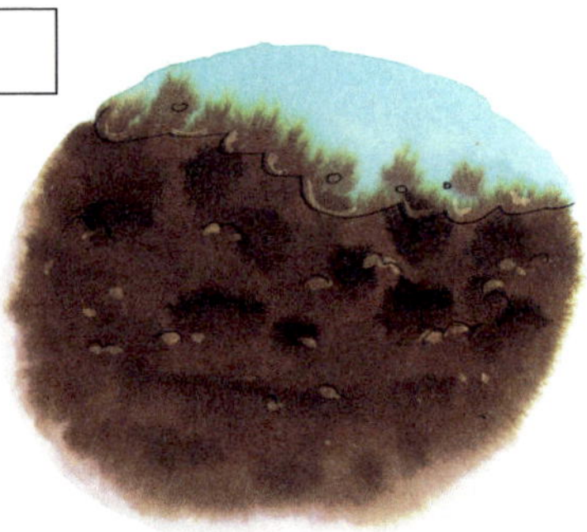

☐

clouds
grass
a tree
a snake
flowers
a tree
grass

☐

☐

☐

Die Reihenfolge eines Inselrundgangs bestimmen, den Inselrundgang beschreiben (◊)

An island puzzle: the pictures

1 Cut out.

An island puzzle: the words

1 Read. Glue the pictures on the right words.

	1	2	3	4	5
A	rainy	cloudy	birds	mountain	sunny
B	flowers	flowers	trees	trees	trees
C	mud	river	river	Ginger	butterfly
D	river	bird	Dr Heal	Dr Heal	chameleon

Wörter lesen und die Puzzlebilder einkleben (◊)

I know these words

bird • butterfly • flower • grass • mountain • rainy • river • sunny • tree

123 **1** Number.

 ☐  ☐  ☐

 ☐  ☐  ☐

 ☐  ☐  ☐

2 Write.

Nature	Weather	Animals

3 Can you write more words?

Bilder in der richtigen Reihenfolge nummerieren, Wörter nach Wortfeldern ordnen (◊)

Portfolio: My photo

1 Read. **2** Draw. **3** Write.

There's grass and a river. Dr Heal is on the grass. There's a butterfly on Dr Heal's toe.

Was ich dazugelernt habe

Datum: ____________

Zeige jetzt noch einmal, was du kannst.
Ich fand die Aufgabe: ☺ leicht 😐 mittel ☹ schwer

1 Ich habe diese Lieder gesungen:
The weather song ☐
Race you down the mountain ☐

2 Ich habe (Name) ____________ gefragt, wie das Wetter heute ist. ☐

3 Ich habe (Name) ____________ gesagt, wie das Wetter heute ist. ☐

4 Ich habe (Name) ____________ diese Wörter genannt:

 ☐  ☐  ☐  ☐

 ☐  ☐  ☐  ☐

Ich kann einige davon auch aufschreiben:

____

____

5 Ich habe (Name) ____________ diese Reime aufgesagt:
I like mud ☐
Don't pick flowers ☐

6 Ich habe (Name) ____________ meinen Inselrundgang vorgestellt. ☐

Ginger's photos from Great Britain

1 Draw.

Nessie in Loch Ness

English roses

Robin Red Breast

The River Thames

Ben Nevis

Stonehenge

2 Write.

My favourite photo is:

____.

Where's the mouse?

1 Write.

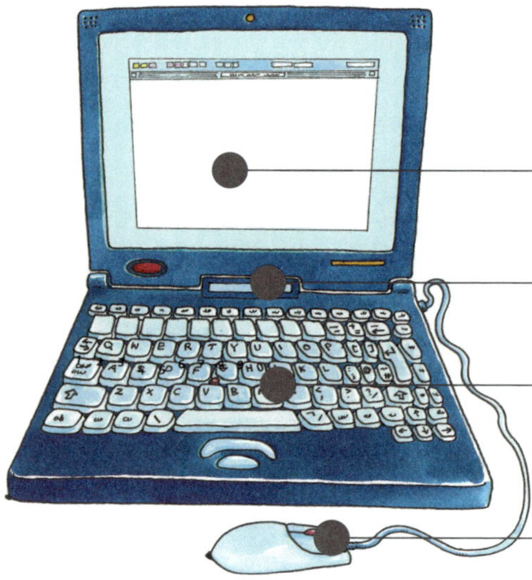

mouse
notebook
window
keyboard

2 Write.

behind • on • under

bed • chair • clock • table

The mouse is

The mouse is

The mouse is

The mouse is

Computerwörter schreiben; aufschreiben, wo sich etwas befindet (◊)

Vehicles in the city

1 Draw.

bikes
buses
cars
motorbikes
planes
trains

2 Write.

There are ____________ buses, ____________,

____________, ____________,

____________ and ____________.

Weitere Fahrzeuge zeichnen, Fahrzeuge zählen und die jeweilige Anzahl aufschreiben (◊)

The way to Professor Bit's house

CD 2.28

1 Listen. Draw a line.

Go to
Turn left
Turn right

2 Write.

________________ ________________ ________________

Professor Bit's workshop

CD 2.31

1 Listen. Tick the boxes.

camera
mobile phone
notebook
radio
skateboard
toaster

2 Write. What is fixed? What is broken?

fixed	broken

Professor Bit's robot

1 Read. Write the numbers.

- [ ] Professor Bit's robot can walk.
- [ ] Professor Bit's robot can clean his desk.
- [ ] Professor Bit's robot can carry his bag.
- [ ] Professor Bit's robot can speak.
- [ ] Professor Bit's robot can open the window.

2 Draw and write.

My robot can ______________________

____

____

____

____

Sätze lesen und in der richtigen Reihenfolge nummerieren (◊)

Portfolio: My dream house

1 Draw your dream house.

Was ich dazugelernt habe

Datum: ____________________

Zeige jetzt noch einmal, was du kannst.
Ich fand die Aufgabe: ☺ leicht 😐 mittel ☹ schwer

◯ **1** Ich habe (Name) ____________________ die englischen Bezeichnungen von Verkehrsmitteln genannt. ☐

Ich kann einige davon auch aufschreiben:

____

____

◯ **2** Ich habe diese Lieder gesungen:
Let's go ☐ My skateboard's broken ☐ The Hokey Cokey ☐

◯ **3** Ich habe (Name) ____________________ einen Weg auf Englisch beschrieben. ☐

◯ **4** Ich habe (Name) ____________________ den Chant „Robot in the bedroom“ aufgesagt. ☐

◯ **5** Ich habe (Name) ____________________ gesagt, dass etwas kaputt ist. ☐

Ich kann dies auch aufschreiben: ____________________

____ ☐

◯ **6** Ich habe mit (Name) ____________________ den Dialog „In a workshop“ gespielt. ☐

◯ **7** Ich habe mein Traumhaus gemalt und es (Name) ____________________ vorgestellt. ☐

◯ **8** Ich habe die Geschichte von „Professor Bit's robot“ gehört. ☐

Portfolio: My favourite book

1 Talk. 2 Draw. 3 Write.

My favourite book is: ______________________________.

A story for Ginger

1 Read. **2** Write.

The Prince is in the castle.
There's a knock on the door.

Prince: Hello, Father. Please come in.
Father: Thank you.
Prince: Hello, Mother. Please come in.
Mother: Thank you.
Prince: Hello, Wolf. Please come in.
Wolf: Thank you.
Prince: Hello, Fairy. Please come in.
Fairy: Thank you.

3 Write the names. Act out.

______________ is the prince. ______________ is the father/king.

______________ is the mother/queen. ______________ is the wolf.

______________ is the fairy.

An invitation to a party

1 Read. **2** Number. **3** Write.

- [1] Ravi: Here's an invitation from Prince Charming.
- [ ] Ravi: Goodbye. See you on Sunday.
- [ ] Ravi: Can you come?
- [ ] LRRH: Goodbye.
- [ ] LRRH: Yes, I can.
- [2] LRRH: Thank you. Oh – a party. Great.

(LRRH = Little Red Riding Hood)

Ravi: Here's an invitation ______________ Prince Charming.

LRRH: ____

______ ____

______ ____

______ ____

______ ____

______ ____

______ ____

______ ____

______ ____

4 Act out.

Clothes

1 Read. **2** Write.

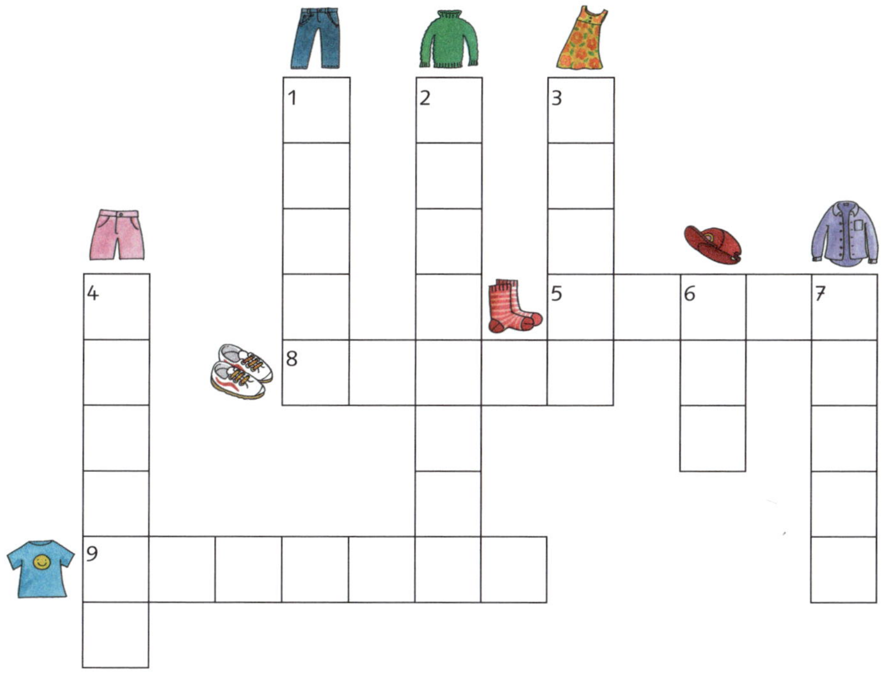

cap
dress
jeans
pullover
shirt
shoes
shorts
socks
T-shirt

3 Write. **4** Draw.

one = c	two = d	three = e	four = h	five = i
six = k	seven = o	eight = r	nine = s	ten = t

10 – 9 4 5 8 10
T – s h i r t

9 4 7 8 10 9
_ _ _ _ _ _

2 8 3 9 9
_ _ _ _ _

9 4 7 3 9
_ _ _ _ _

9 7 1 6 9
_ _ _ _ _

9 4 5 8 10
_ _ _ _ _

How are you?

1 Read. **2** Write. **3** Draw.

happy
sad
scared
angry

Portfolio: My wish

1 Read. 2 Write.

bag • book • cap • comic • dress • jeans • prince • shoes • shorts • wolf

I want a bag,
a ________ and a ________.

I want ________,
________ and ________.

I want a ________,
a ________ and a ________.

I ________
a ________.

3 Draw. 4 Write.

I want ________
____
____
____
____
____
____

Sätze in den Sprechblasen ergänzen; ein Bild malen und beschreiben (◊)

Was ich dazugelernt habe

Datum: ____________________

Zeige jetzt noch einmal, was du kannst.
Ich fand die Aufgabe: ☺ leicht 😐 mittel ☹ schwer

◯ **1** Ich habe diese Lieder gesungen:
Skidamarink ☐ For he's a jolly good fellow ☐
Pick it up ☐ Who's afraid of the big bad wolf? ☐

◯ **2** Ich habe (Name) ____________________ zu meiner Party eingeladen und gesagt, wann die Party stattfindet. ☐

◯ **3** Ich habe (Name) ____________________ den Reim „I paint my fingernails" aufgesagt. ☐

◯ **4** Ich habe (Name) ____________________ gesagt, was ich mir von einer Fee wünsche. ☐

◯ **5** Ich habe (Name) ____________________ gesagt, wer die Märchenfiguren sind.

 ☐  ☐  ☐  ☐  ☐

◯ **6** Ich habe (Name) ____________________ gesagt, welche Kleidung ich heute anhabe. ☐

Ich kann einige Kleidungsstücke auch aufschreiben:

____

◯ **7** Ich habe (Name) ____________________ mein Cinderella-Märchenbuch vorgestellt. ☐

Cinderella

1 Cut out.

Halloween

1 Read.

2 Write.

ghost • jack-o'-lantern • skeleton • vampire • witch

____________ ____________ ____________ ____________

I like the ______________________ best.

3 Talk.

4 Draw.

Happy Halloween!

A Christmas card

1 Write.

a • and • Dear • From,
Happy New Year. • Merry Christmas

Breakfast

Fruit

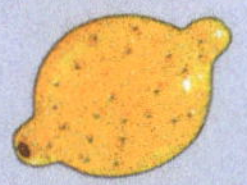

Sandwiches

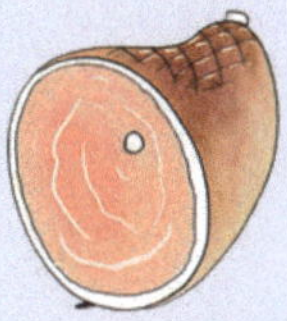

Word fields

Animals

Weather

Nature

Vehicles

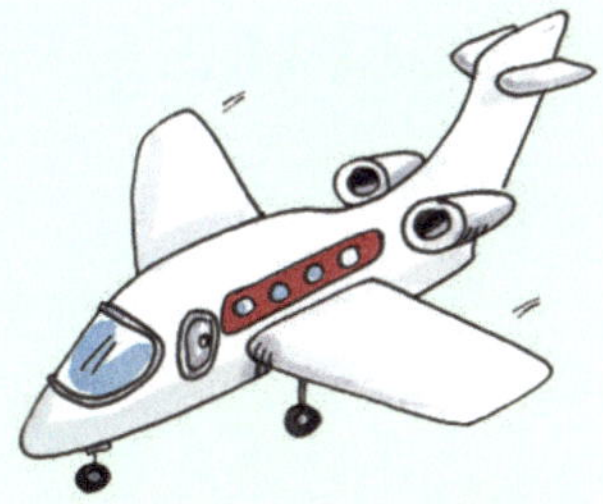

House

Clothes

School things

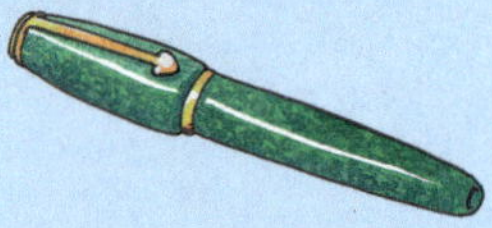

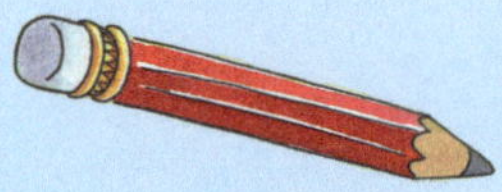

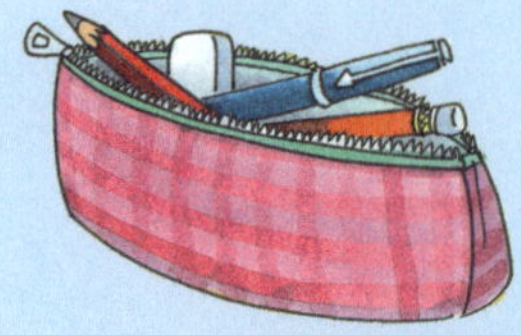

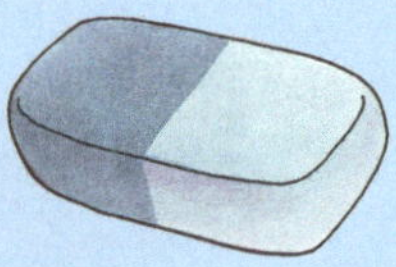

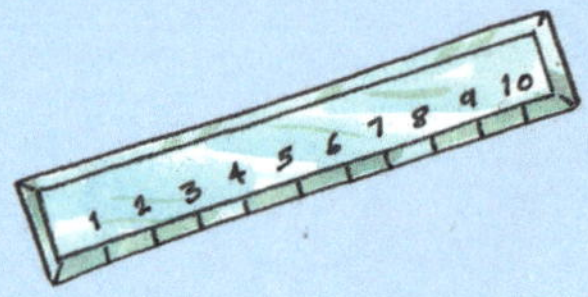

Family

Parts of the body